Count Your Way through the
Arab World

by Jim Haskins

illustrations by Dana Gustafson

Carolrhoda Books, Inc./Minneapolis

To Elisa Beth and the future

LIBRARY OF CONGRESS CATALOGING-IN-PUBLICATION DATA

Haskins, James, 1941-
   Count your way through the Arab world.

   Summary: Uses Arabic numerals from one to ten to
introduce concepts about Arab countries and Arab
culture.
   1. Arab countries—Juvenile literature.   2. Arabic
language—Numerals—Juvenile literature. [1. Arab
countries.   2. Counting]   I. Gustafson, Dana, ill.
II. Title.
DS36.7.H38   1987   909'.0974927   87-6391
ISBN 0-87616-304-4 (lib. bdg.)

Manufactured in the United States of America

1 2 3 4 5 6 7 8 9 10 97 96 95 94 93 92 91 90 89 88 87

Introductory Note

Arabic is the language of over 185 million people who live throughout North Africa and the Middle East. Written Arabic is basically the same for all of these people, but there are many different dialects (variations of speech) in spoken Arabic. The pronunciation guide for this book uses the most widely understood dialect, the Egyptian dialect.

There are 28 letters in the Arabic alphabet. They are all consonants. Vowels are shown by small marks above and below the consonants. Arabic is written from right to left, the opposite of English.

Almost all Arabic-speaking people are Muslims, followers of the Islamic faith. Islam is a religion that follows the teachings of a man called Muhammad, who was born around A.D. 570. Muslims believe that Muhammad was a prophet, a messenger of God. The holy book of Islam, the Koran, is a collection of teachings and rules that Muslims follow. Most of the laws and customs of Arabic-speaking peoples are based on Islam.

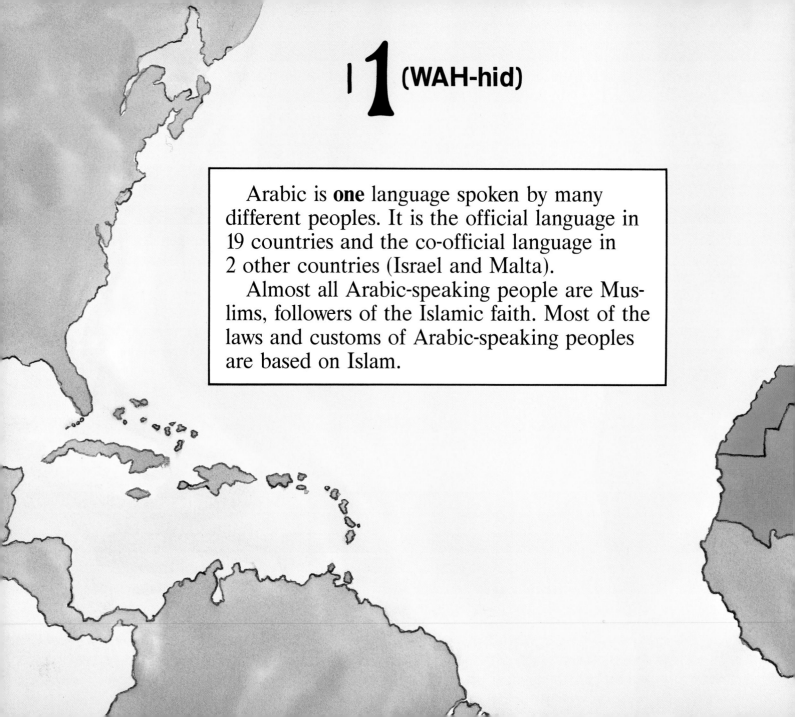

1 (WAH-hid)

Arabic is **one** language spoken by many different peoples. It is the official language in 19 countries and the co-official language in 2 other countries (Israel and Malta).

Almost all Arabic-speaking people are Muslims, followers of the Islamic faith. Most of the laws and customs of Arabic-speaking peoples are based on Islam.

٢ 2 (it-NAYN)

Tents with **two** rooms separated by a curtain are home to most Bedouins, Arabs who travel and live in the desert areas of the Middle East. One of the rooms is used by the men and is also used for receiving guests. The other room is for the women and their possessions.

The Bedouins are independent people. They are nomads, travelers without permanent homes, who herd their sheep and goats in search of grazing land and water. Although most Bedouins continue to be nomadic, more Bedouins live in towns and villages today than ever before.

ﻣ **3** (tah-LAH-tah)

"The Bird of the Golden Feather" is a folktale from Syria about **three** princes. In this tale, all three princes search for a bird that has feathers of pure gold. Traveling together they come upon a smooth stone on which is carved:

> This way lies the Road of the Burning
> This way lies the Road of the Drowning
> This way lies the Road of No Returning

Each brother takes a different path and each has many adventures.

There are hundreds of Arab folktales. Many of them begin with these words: "This happened, or maybe it did not. The time is long past, and much is forgot."

 **4** (ar-BAH-ah)

The Koran, the holy book of Islam, states that a man may have as many as **four** wives. Being married to more than one woman at a time is called polygamy. Polygamy is much less commonly practiced in the Arab world today than in past times.

According to Islamic tradition, men and women have very separate roles in life. The rules of the Islamic religion allow women influence over family matters, including partial control over family money, but they do not allow women to be involved in public life. Although many women in the Arab world still follow these rules, more and more women are now going to school and working outside the home.

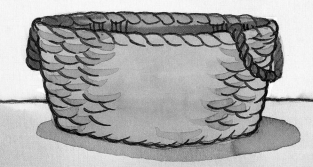

5

△ **(KAHM-sah)**

At least **five** times a day, all Muslims must face the holy city of Mecca in Saudi Arabia and pray. In this way, the faithful are able to remember God, even when they are busy.

This is not hard for Muslims to do when they are in an Arab country, where prayer timetables are published or broadcast. (Daily prayer times change every day according to the times of the sunrise and sunset.) When Muslims are in non-Arab countries, however,

it is hard for them to know when to pray and in which direction to face.

An electrical engineer from Egypt solved this problem by inventing a "prayer clock." It is an alarm clock with a built-in computer that is able to figure out the five daily prayer times each day. The alarm buzzes five times a day, once at each prayer hour. The clock also has a compass that can be set to point toward Mecca.

The Arab world includes many desert countries, and the camel, being a desert animal, is necessary to the lives of many Arabs. There are **six** reasons why the camel is so important to Arabs who live in the desert. People (1) drink its milk and (2) eat its meat. They (3) make tents and clothing from its hide and (4) burn

its dung as fuel. The camel is (5) sometimes used as money in trading goods with other people. Most important of all, the camel is (6) the ship of the desert, able to carry heavy loads and passengers 40 miles or more a day over the desert sands.

V 7 (SAHB-ah)

The Koran states that all able Muslims must make a pilgrimage to Mecca at least once in their lifetime. When they get there, they must walk around the Kaaba **seven** times and kiss the sacred Black Stone in its wall.

The Kaaba is the holiest shrine of the Islamic religion and has been worshipped by Muslims for many, many centuries. According to Islamic beliefs, the Black Stone within one of its walls was made sacred by Muhammad's touch in A.D. 630.

∧ 8 (ta-MAHN-ya)

In Arabic, there are **eight** different ways to say cousin. Each way describes the exact relationship of that person to his or her family. A male cousin, then, can be introduced in one of four different ways:

ibn AHMM	ibn AHMM-eh
father's brother's son	father's sister's son
ibn KAHL	ibn KAHL-eh
mother's brother's son	mother's sister's son

A female cousin can also be introduced in one of four different ways:

bent AHMM
 father's brother's daughter

bent AHMM-eh
 father's sister's daughter

bent KAHL
 mother's brother's daughter

bent KAHL-eh
 mother's sister's daughter

In a Muslim town, the market is second in importance only to the mosque. There are **nine** major kinds of goods and services available in a Muslim market, and they are always arranged in order of importance in the following way: Inside the town walls are (1) dealers of religious objects (candles, incense, and perfumes);

(2) booksellers and bookbinders; (3) leather merchants and slipper makers; (4) textile merchants; (5) carpenters, locksmiths, and coppersmiths; (6) blacksmiths; (7) tanners and dyers. Outside the town walls are (8) potters; (9) singers and storytellers.

I·**10** (AH-shah-rah)

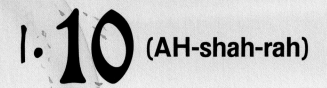

Sand dunes in many Arab countries are huge hills of sand that can extend for as many as **ten** miles.

The golden sand contains grains of many different colors—red, gold, silver, purple, and brown. In Saudi Arabia, the months of May, June, and July make up the sandstorm season, when strong winds swirl the sand around and around. During this time, people often have to cover their faces in order to see or to breathe.

Pronunciation Guide

1 / ١ / WAH-hid

2 / ٢ / it-NAYN

3 / ٣ / tah-LAH-tah

4 / ٤ / ar-BAH-ah

5 / ٥ / KAHM-sah

6 / ٦ / SIHT-tah

7 / ٧ / SAHB-ah

8 / ٨ / tah-MAHN-yah

9 / ٩ / TIHS-ah

10 / ١٠ / AH-shah-rah